CONVERSATIONAL GERMAN DIALOGUES

OVER 100 CONVERSATIONS AND SHORT STORIES TO LEARN THE GERMAN LANGUAGE. GROW YOUR VOCABULARY WHILST HAVING FUN WITH DAILY USED PHRASES AND LANGUAGE LEARNING LESSONS!

LANGUAGE MASTERY

Copyright © 2022 by Language Mastery

All rights reserved.

No part of this book may be reproduced in any form or by any electronic or mechanical means, including information storage and retrieval systems, without written permission from the author, except for the use of brief quotations in a book review.

CONTENTS

Introduction ... vii

1. THE BIRTHDAY GIFT ... 1
   Emotions
   Summary ... 4
   Words to Remember ... 4
   Questions ... 5
   Answers ... 6
   English Translation ... 7

2. THE FINAL CHOICE ... 11
   Present Tense Verbs
   Summary ... 14
   Words to Remember ... 14
   Questions ... 15
   Answers ... 16
   English Translation ... 17

3. HIDE AND SEEK ... 21
   House And Furniture
   Summary ... 26
   Words to Remember ... 26
   Questions ... 27
   Answers ... 29
   English Translation ... 29

4. THE SEARCH ... 35
   Question Words
   Summary ... 39
   Words to Remember ... 40
   Questions ... 40

Answers	42
English Translation	42

5. THE WEEKEND
Likes & Dislikes

47

Summary	51
Words to Remember	51
Questions	52
Answers	53
English Translation	54

6. THE ADVENTURE
Prepositions + To Be/To Have

59

Summary	62
Words to Remember	62
Questions	64
Answers	65
English Translation	65
Conclusion	69
Also by Language Mastery	73

INTRODUCTION

Language is an irreplaceable part of human life. Just imagine for a moment that you wake up one morning and cannot speak your own language. How would your life be? How would you feel? Wouldn't life feel like a total mess? While knowing a language is essential, knowing more than one could be a competitive advantage for you. You will be able to communicate easily with more people and this can help you greatly in improving the quality of both your personal as well as professional life. What's more? Learning a new language is excellent for your brain. It is like a workout for the mind and can help you stay younger mentally.

Learning a new language isn't as hard as it seems. Learning can take place outside the classroom too. All you need is patience, lots of hard work, and regular practice. This book can be your guiding light and helping hand that you need on your language learning journey.

CREATED FOR BEGINNERS

This book is geared toward beginners. You will learn a new language through the adventures of Jack and Rose, a young British boy and a Swiss girl. It is divided into 17 chapters. As you walk with them through their various life experiences, you will not only be thoroughly entertained but will also get to learn loads of commonly used phrases and words to enrich your vocabulary.

This book can provide you with a really fun learning experience and will immerse you into a new language in the most interesting way.

THE BENEFITS OF LEARNING A NEW LANGUAGE

Learning a language is one of the most complete cognitive exercises: memory is activated while new neural connections are formed as we move from one language to another. Studying a foreign language increases language, reasoning, abstraction, and calculation skills. In addition to this, knowing more than one language opens up a whole new world to you: from being able to communicate with a larger audience, or opening your access to new job opportunities and relationships.

HOW TO USE THIS BOOK

Each chapter is divided into five sections. The first section contains the story. This is followed by a brief summary of the story. Next, you will find a list of important words that you must remember to increase your fluency, efficiency, and flow with this new language. Following this will be a section containing five questions based on the story. The final section will have answers to these questions. Whether you are 15 or 55, learning a new language using this book is going to be extremely easy and interesting.

Start by reading the story. Don't pressure yourself too much and just try to understand and absorb as much as you can in your first read. It is normal to not be able to understand every word. You are learning a new language after all. Read the summary next to confirm your understanding of the story. Try to remember the words/phrases listed under the "words to remember" category. Finally, check your knowledge and understanding by trying to answer the questions at the end of every chapter. Check your solutions with the answer key provided to see how many questions you got right. Try to learn from your mistakes and move on to the next chapter. As you progress from one chapter to the next, you will see your grasp of the new language gradually improve.

READ AND LISTEN

We highly recommend you buy the audio version of this book. If you choose to listen to the audiobook, you will hear a native English speaker narrating each story before or during reading. Reading along will help you become accustomed to their accent, which will be helpful when applying your new language skills in real-life situations.

Don't wait anymore. Put all your fears and apprehension away and set foot on this amazing language learning journey today!

1

THE BIRTHDAY GIFT
EMOTIONS

Jack ist ganz allein auf den Straßen des kleinen Dorfes. Der Mann in Uniform kehrt nach dem Frühstück zu seiner Arbeit bei der Bahn zurück. Jack hat den ganzen Tag nichts zu tun, also beschließt er, ein Geschenk für Kathryns Geburtstagsparty einzukaufen. Kathryn und Jack sind seit ihrer Kindheit befreundet, aber für Jack ist Kathryn mehr als nur eine Freundin. Er ist heimlich in sie verliebt, aber Kathryn weiß nichts von seinen Gefühlen. Er liebt sie, aber er ist **nervös** und **ängstlich** darüber, seine Zuneigung zum Ausdruck zu bringen. Er befürchtet, dass sie „nein" sagen könnte. Er erfährt von einem guten Geschäft an der Landstraße außerhalb des Dorfes und beschließt, dorthin zu gehen.

Jack ist **begeistert**, bald zu Kathryns Geburtstagsfeier zu gehen. Er erreicht den Laden und sein Blick fällt auf ein Plakat. Ihm gefällt das Kleid auf dem Plakat; und das Mädchen, das es trägt, sieht Kathryn auch sehr ähnlich. Also geht Jack auf der Suche nach demselben Kleid in den Laden. Er ist sehr **zuversichtlich**, dass es Kathryn gefallen wird. Der Laden ist riesig. Es hat vier Etagen und auf dem Schild über der Ladentür steht "Herr und Frau

Stolz". Er ist **überrascht**, an diesem abgelegenen Ort einen so eleganten Laden zu sehen.

„Entschuldigen Sie bitte", sagt er und geht auf das Verkaufspersonal zu. „Wo kann ich das Kleid finden, das draußen auf dem Plakat zu sehen ist?"

Die Frau sieht sehr **wütend** und **gelangweilt** aus. Sie sagt nichts und zeigt nur auf den Fahrstuhl. Jack nimmt an, dass sich das Kleid im ersten Stock befindet, also dreht er sich um und geht zum Aufzug. Er drückt auf den Knopf und wartet. Um den Fahrstuhl herum liegen viele Bücher. Jack liest die Titel und ein Buch erregt seine Aufmerksamkeit. Er geht näher und nimmt es aus dem Regal. Der Titel lautet: "Sie **interessieren** sich für eine Frau, wissen aber nicht, wie Sie es ihr sagen sollen? Lies mich." Jack **hofft**, dass ihm dieses Buch helfen wird. Er beschließt, es zu kaufen.

Der Aufzug kommt und die Türen öffnen sich. Er geht hinein und zwei junge Mädchen folgen ihm. Die Türen des Aufzugs schließen sich und in diesem Moment klingelt Jacks Handy. Es ist ein Videoanruf von Kathryn. Jack ist äußerst **glücklich**. Er heckt schnell einen Plan aus, um zu testen, was Kathryn für ihn empfindet. Er geht ans Telefon und vergewissert sich, dass eines der beiden Mädchen im Aufzug im Videoanruf zu sehen ist.

„Wenn Kathryn sich nach diesem Mädchen erkundigt, bedeutet das, dass sie **eifersüchtig** ist. Und wenn sie eifersüchtig ist, bedeutet das, dass sie mich auch heimlich liebt", denkt sich Jack.

Kathryn ist **zornig**, weil sie denkt, dass Jack nicht an ihrer Geburtstagsfeier teilnehmen wird. Jack spricht liebevoll mit ihr und versichert ihr, dass er bei der Feier dabei sein wird. Jack erzählt ihr von den Abenteuern seiner Reise und sie ist **amüsiert**. Sie scheint nicht einmal ein kleines bisschen **neugierig** zu sein, wer das Mädchen ist.

Das macht Jack ein bisschen **traurig** und er zieht sich für einen Moment zurück, aber bald fasst er sich und entschließt sich, das perfekte Geschenk für seine besondere Frau zu **finden**.

Die Türen des Fahrstuhls öffnen sich und die beiden Mädchen steigen aus. Jack folgt ihnen einfach, ohne viel auf die Umgebung zu achten. Seine ganze Aufmerksamkeit gilt Kathryns WhatsApp-Profilbild. Das Bild zeigt Kathryn zusammen mit einem Jungen und zwei Mädchen, und die Anwesenheit des Jungen macht Jack sehr **neidisch**. Jack kann das nicht ertragen und ist **entschlossen** herauszufinden, wer dieser Junge ist.

„Lass mich ihn auf Instagram finden", denkt er sich und beginnt die Suche.

Er geht weiter und sucht gleichzeitig den Jungen auf Instagram. Plötzlich ruft ihm eine Frauenstimme zu. Sie ist eine Verkäuferin hier.

"Entschuldigen Sie bitte! Dies ist ein Bereich nur für Frauen. Suchen Sie jemanden?"

Jack sieht auf und ist extrem **verlegen** und **beschämt**. Er entschuldigt sich schnell bei der Frau und verlässt die Etage.

"Oh Gott! Das war so **dumm**", denkt sich Jack.

Alle anderen Kunden auf dieser Etage sind wütend auf die Verkäuferin. Sie beschweren sich bei ihrem Manager über sie. Der Manager wird sauer auf sie und Jack fühlt sich sehr schuldig wegen der Situation, in die er sie gebracht hat.

Er fasst sich und ohne von irgendetwas **abgelenkt** zu sein, geht er zurück zum Fahrstuhl. Er denkt immer noch an den Jungen auf Kathryns Profilbild. Er ist **verstört** und **hat Angst**, sie zu verlieren.

SUMMARY

Jack geht in ein Geschäft in der Nähe des Dorfes, um ein Geburtstagsgeschenk für Kathryn zu kaufen. Er ist in sie verliebt. Ihm gefällt ein Kleid auf einem Plakat vor dem Laden und er beschließt, es für Kathryn zu kaufen. Als er das Kleid im Laden sucht, landet er ohne sein Wissen in einem Bereich, zu dem nur Frauen Zutritt haben. Der Grund für Jacks Unachtsamkeit ist seine Eifersucht. Er bemerkt einen Jungen auf Kathryns WhatsApp-Profilbild und ist darüber verzweifelt.

WORDS TO REMEMBER

1. **Interessiert** - Interested
2. **Gelangweilt** - Bored
3. **Glücklich** - Happy
4. **Ängstlich** - Anxious
5. **Nervös** - Nervous
6. **Zuversichtlich** - Confident
7. **Begeistert** - Excited
8. **Verstört** - unsettled
9. **Wütend** - Angry
10. **Abgelenkt** - Distracted
11. **Traurig** - Sad
12. **Beschämt** - Ashamed
13. **Verlegen** - Embarrassed
14. **Überrascht** - Surprised
15. **Hoffen** - to hope
16. **Neugierig** - Curious
17. **Amüsiert** - Amused

18. **Eifersüchtig** - Jealous
19. **Neidisch** - Envious
20. **Zornig** - Enraged
21. **Dumm** - Stupid
22. **Entschlossen** - Determined
23. **Stolz** - Proud
24. **Angst haben** – To be afraid

QUESTIONS

1. Wie heißt der Laden, den Jack besucht?

- a. Herr und Frau Pompous
- b. Welt der Frau
- c. Das Kleiderkönigreich
- d. Herr und Frau Stolz

2. Was sieht Jack außerhalb des Ladens?

- a. Einen Wagen
- b. Ein Mann
- c. Ein Essensstand
- d. Ein Plakat

3. Was möchte Jack für Kathryn kaufen?

- a. Schuhe
- b. Eine Handtasche

- c. Ein Kleid
- d. Haarklammern

4. Wer ruft Jack an?

- a. Rose
- b. Seine Mutter
- c. Kathryn
- d. Sein Chef

5. Was beschließt Jack, sich zu kaufen, während er auf den Fahrstuhl wartet?

- a. Ein Buch
- b. Einen Stift
- c. Ein Handy
- d. Eine Sonnenbrille

―――

ANSWERS

1. **d.** Herr und Frau Stolz
2. **d.** Ein Plakat
3. **c.** Ein Kleid
4. **c.** Kathryn
5. **a.** Ein Buch

―――

ENGLISH TRANSLATION

Jack is all alone on the streets of the little village. The man in the uniform returns to his work in the railways after breakfast. Jack has nothing to do all day, so he decides to go gift shopping for Kathryn's birthday party. Kathryn and Jack have been friends since childhood, but for Jack, Kathryn is more than a friend. He is secretly in love with her, but Kathryn is unaware of his feelings for her. He loves her but he's nervous and anxious about expressing his affection. He fears that she might say "no." He finds out about a good store on the highway outside the village and decides to go there.

Jack is very excited about Kathryn's birthday. He reaches the store, and his eyes fall on a poster. He loves the dress in the poster and the girl wearing it also looks very similar to Kathryn. So Jack goes inside the store in search of the same dress. He's very confident that Kathryn will like it. The store is huge. It has four floors and the nameplate outside reads, Mr. and Mrs. Proud. He is surprised to see such a plush store in that remote place.

"Excuse me," he says walking towards the sales staff. "Where can I see the dress which is on the poster outside?"

The woman looks very angry and bored. She says nothing and just points towards the elevator. Jack assumes the dress is on the first floor, so he turns around and starts walking towards the elevator. He pushes the button and waits. Around the elevator are a large number of books. Jack reads the titles and one book captures his attention. He goes closer and picks it up from the shelf. The title reads, Interested in a woman but don't know how to say it? Read me. Jack is hopeful that this book will be of help to him. He decides to buy it.

The elevator arrives and the doors open. He walks in

and two young girls follow him. The doors of the elevator close and at that instance, Jack's phone rings. It's a video call from Kathryn. Jack is super happy. He hatches a quick plan to test what Kathryn feels for him. He answers the phone and makes sure one of the two girls in the elevator is in his frame.

"If Kathryn enquires about this girl, that means she's jealous. And if she is jealous, it means she secretly loves me as well," Jack thinks to himself.

Kathryn is enraged because she is under the impression that Jack will not be attending her birthday party. Jack speaks to her in a loving tone and assures her that he will be there for the party. Jack narrates the adventures of his journey to her and she is amused. She doesn't seem even a tad curious to know about the girl. This makes Jack a bit sad and he momentarily becomes withdrawn, but he soon composes himself and embarks on finding that perfect gift for his special woman.

The doors of the elevator open, and the two girls step out. Jack simply follows them without paying much attention to the surroundings. His entire concentration is centered on Kathryn's WhatsApp display picture. The picture contains Kathryn along with a boy and two girls, and the presence of the boy makes Jack very envious. Jack cannot stand this and he's determined to find out who that boy is.

"Let me hunt him down on Instagram," he thinks to himself and begins his search.

He continues walking and searching simultaneously. Suddenly, a woman's voice calls out to him. She is the sales staff there.

"Excuse me, sir! This is a women-only area. Are you looking for someone?"

Jack looks up, and he's extremely embarrassed and

ashamed. He quickly apologizes to the woman and leaves the floor.

"Oh, God! That was so stupid," Jack thinks to himself.

All the other customers on that floor or angry at the sales staff. They start complaining about her to her manager. The manager gets mad at her and Jack feels very guilty about the position he's put her in.

He composes himself and without allowing himself to get distracted by anything, he gets back to the elevator. The man in Kathryn's display picture is still on his mind. He's disturbed and very afraid that he might lose her.

2
THE FINAL CHOICE
PRESENT TENSE VERBS

Jack ist immer noch im Laden. Er möchte unbedingt ein tolles Geschenk für Kathryns Geburtstag **kaufen** und es gibt keinen anderen Laden in der Nähe. Er kehrt ins Erdgeschoss zurück. Er möchte gerne in jedes Stockwerk **gehen** und **sich umschauen**.

"Was möchten Sie **sehen**?", fragt eine blonde Verkäuferin Jack.

Jack geht zur Theke, wo die Frau ist. Es gibt eine Reihe von Düften im Regal in schönen Flakons in verschiedenen Formen. Dort im Regal steht eine Reihe von Düften in schönen Flakons verschiedener Formen. Jack mag die Formen. Er nimmt eine Flasche, die die Form einer Rosenblüte hat, um den Duft zu **riechen**.

„Sie können den Tester **probieren**. Was Sie in der Hand haben, ist ein neuer Artikel. Kunden dürfen diese vor dem Kauf nicht **verwenden**", sagt die Frau zu Jack und **gibt** ihm einen Tester.

Jack nimmt den Tester und sprüht etwas auf seine Hand. Der Geruch ist himmlisch. Jack möchte den Preis **wissen**, bevor er sich entscheidet. Er nimmt die neue

Flasche, um den Preis zu sehen, aber dort wird kein Preis erwähnt.

"Wie viel kostet dieser Duft?", **fragt** er die Frau.

„Er kostet 150 Euro", sagt sie ihm.

Jack **denkt**, dass das teuer ist. Plötzlich **hört** er sanfte Musik aus der Flasche spielen.

„Kann diese Flasche Musik **machen**?", fragt Jack überrascht.

"Jawohl. Die Musik spielt, wenn Sie den Deckel **berühren**", sagt sie.

Jack berührt den Deckel und die Musik beginnt zu spielen. Er **fühlt** sich gut mit der Flasche.

„**Verwendet** das Batterien?", fragt Jack.

"Nein, dies ist eine neue Technologie. Solange sich Parfüm in der Flasche befindet, spielt die Musik jedes Mal, wenn Sie den Deckel berühren. Wenn Sie zu uns zurück**kommen**, wenn Ihre Flasche leer ist, können wir sie wieder für Sie auffüllen", antwortet sie.

„Aber ich lebe in Großbritannien!"

"Keine Bange. Sie brauchen uns nur **anrufen** und wir schicken Ihnen einen Nachfüllpack per Post zu. Sie können es ganz einfach selbst **auffüllen**. Es ist ganz leicht."

"Das ist großartig! Aber es ist sehr teuer. Haben Sie ein Rabattangebot?"

„Im Moment nicht", antwortet die Frau.

"OK. Können Sie das bitte für mich **aufbewahren**? Ich möchte mir die restlichen Produkte im Laden ansehen, bevor ich mich entscheide", **sagt** Jack zu der Frau.

Er geht weiter und findet Regale voller Schönheitsprodukte für Frauen. Es gibt Nagellacke, Lippenstifte und eine Vielzahl anderer Kosmetikprodukte. Jack ist verwirrt. Er hat keine Ahnung von Make-up. Er versucht, die Produkte zu **verstehen**, indem er die Etiketten liest, aber es fällt ihm sehr schwer, das richtige auszu**wählen**.

Dann geht Jack in die erste Etage. Die Verkäuferin begleitet ihn. Er bemerkt, dass er zuvor noch nicht auf dieser Etage war.

„Das war der vierte Stock. Es ist ein Schönheitssalon und Spa nur für Frauen", **erzählt** die Verkäuferin, bevor Jack etwas sagt.

Jack lächelt und **geht** weiter. Die Etage ist voll von schönen Kleidern. Jack ist fasziniert. Er **wird** sehr aufgeregt, als er dasteht und sich Kathryn in all diesen Kleidern vorstellt. Er schaut sich sorgfältig um, ob er das Kleid von dem Plakat außerhalb des Ladens **finden** kann. Nach einigem Suchen sieht er endlich genau das Kleid.

„Das ist es, wonach ich gesucht habe. Ich **brauche** eine kleine Größe von diesem Kleid, bitte", sagt Jack.

„Selbstverständlich", sagt die Frau und **bringt** eine kleine Größe für Jack aus dem Lagerraum. „Ist das alles? Oder möchten Sie noch etwas kaufen?"

"Nein. Das ist alles. Ich **nehme** das Parfum und dieses Kleid."

"Gute Entscheidung!"

„Und auch viel Geld! Aber es ist okay. Sie wird sich sehr freuen", sagt Jack.

„Ist es jemand Besonderes?", fragt die Frau mit einem breiten Lächeln.

Jack lächelt charmant und nickt.

„Dann packe ich es Ihnen hübsch als Geschenk ein", sagt die Frau mit einem Augenzwinkern.

Jack bezahlt und sieht zu, wie die Verkäuferin die Geschenke kreativ in Hochglanzpapier einpackt.

SUMMARY

Jack geht durch den Laden und sucht nach einem Geschenk für Kathryn. Mit der Hilfe einer blonden Verkäuferin findet er ein tolles Parfüm, aber sein Herz hängt immer noch an dem Kleid vom Plakat. Nach einigem Suchen findet er das Kleid und freut sich über die wunderbaren Geschenke für Kathryn.

WORDS TO REMEMBER

1. **Sehen** - to look
2. **Machen** - to make
3. **Bringen** - to bring
4. **Kaufen** - to buy
5. **Finden** - to find
6. **Werden** - to become
7. **Sagen** - to say
8. **Erzählen** - to tell
9. **Fragen** - to ask
10. **Umschauen** - to look around
11. **Hören** - to hear
12. **Riechen** - to smell
13. **Berühren** - to touch
14. **Nehmen** - to take
15. **Verstehen** - to understand
16. **Wählen** - to choose
17. **Fühlen** - to feel
18. **Arbeiten** - to work
19. **Behalten** - to keep
20. **Versuchen** - to try

21. **Möchten** - to want
22. **Denken** - to think
23. **Benutzen** - to use
24. **Wissen** - to know
25. **Geben** - to give
26. **Kommen** - to come
27. **Anrufen** - to call
28. **Machen** - to do
29. **Brauchen** - to need
30. **Gehen** - to go

QUESTIONS

1. Wer hilft Jack beim Einkaufen?

- a. Eine blonde Frau
- b. Eine schöne Frau
- c. Ein alter Mann
- d. Ein junger Mann

2. Welche Form hat das Parfüm, das Jack wählt?

- a. Rund
- b. Rosenblüte
- c. Quadratisch
- d. Tasche

3. Was ist einzigartig an dem Parfüm?

- a. Es ist billig
- b. Es macht Musik
- c. Es ist teuer
- d. Es ist automatisch

4. Wo findet Jack das Kleid auf dem Plakat?

- a. In der ersten Etage des Ladens
- b. In der zweiten Etage des Ladens
- c. In der dritten Etage des Ladens
- d. In der vierten Etage des Ladens

5. Was macht die blonde Frau am Ende mit den Geschenken?

- a. Sie schickt sie an Kathryn
- b. Sie wickelt sie in Hochglanzpapier ein
- c. Sie weigert sich, sie an Jack zu verkaufen
- d. Sie zerstört sie

ANSWERS

1. **a.** Eine blonde Frau
2. **b.** Rosenblüte
3. **b.** Es macht Musik
4. **a.** In der ersten Etage des Ladens
5. **b.** Sie wickelt sie in Hochglanzpapier ein

ENGLISH TRANSLATION

Jack is still at the store. He desperately wants to buy an amazing gift for Kathryn's birthday and there is no other store around. He returns back to the ground floor and decides to look around each floor.

"What would you like to see sir?" a blond saleswoman asks Jack.

Jack walks towards the counter where the woman is. There are a number of fragrances on the shelf in beautiful bottles of different shapes. Jack likes the shapes. He picks up one bottle that is in the shape of a rose flower to smell the fragrance.

"You can try the tester sir. What you have in your hand is a new piece. Customers are not allowed to use these before purchase," the woman tells Jack and gives him the tester.

Jack takes the tester and sprays a little on his hand. The smell is heavenly. Jack wants to know the price before he can decide. He picks up the new bottle to see the price, but there is no mention of it there.

"What is the price of this one?" he asks the woman.

"This costs €150," she tells him.

Jack thinks it's expensive. He suddenly hears soft music playing from the bottle.

"Is this a musical bottle?" Jack asks in surprise.

"Yes, sir. Music plays when you touch the lid," she says.

Jack touches the lid and the music starts playing. He feels good about the bottle.

"Does this use batteries?" Jack enquires.

"No, sir. This is a new technology. As long as there is perfume in the bottle, the music will play every time you touch the lid. If you come back to us once your bottle is empty, we can refill it for you," she replies.

"But I live in the UK!"

"No worries. Just call us, and we will send you a refill pack by mail. You can easily fill it up yourself. It is very easy."

"This is amazing! But it's very expensive. Do you have a discount offer?"

"Not at the moment," the woman replies.

"Ok. Please keep this aside for me. I want to have a look at the rest of the products in the store before I make the final call," Jack says to the woman.

He walks ahead and finds shelves full of beauty products for women. There are nail varnishes, lipsticks, and a host of other cosmetic products. Jack is confused. He knows nothing about makeup. He tries to understand the products by reading the labels, but he finds it very difficult to choose the right one.

Jack then goes to the first floor. The saleswoman accompanies him. He realizes he was not on this floor previously.

"That was the fourth floor, sir. It's a women's only beauty salon and spa," the saleswoman explains before Jack says anything.

Jack smiles and moves ahead. The area is full of beautiful dresses. Jack is mesmerized. He becomes very excited as he stands there imagining Kathryn in all those dresses. He looks around carefully to see if he can find the dress from the poster outside of the store. After a bit of searching, he finally sees the exact dress.

"This is what I have been looking for. I need a small size in this dress, please," Jack says.

"Sure, sir," the woman says and brings a small size for

Jack from the storeroom. "Will this be all? Or are you looking to buy something more?"

"No. That's about it. The perfume and this dress.".

"Good choice!"

"And a lot of money too! But it's fine. She'll be very happy," Jack says.

"Is it someone special?" the woman asks with a wide smile.

Jack smiles charmingly and nods.

"Then I will give you a beautiful gift wrap," the woman says with a wink.

Jack makes the payment and watches as the saleswoman creatively wraps the gifts in glossy paper.

3
HIDE AND SEEK
HOUSE AND FURNITURE

Rose, die Lehrerin und ihre zwölf Vorschulkinder sind im **Haus** des Anwalts. Sie sind alle um einen **Tisch** im **Wohnzimmer** versammelt. Ihre Augen sind auf die Hand des Anwalts gerichtet. Er zeigt ihnen einen Zaubertrick. Die Kinder interessieren sich sehr für den Trick.

„Ich werde jetzt diese Münzen in meiner Hand auf den Teppich fallen lassen. Achtet auf die Münzen. Behaltet sie im Auge, während sie aus meiner Hand auf den **Teppich** fallen", sagt der Anwalt.

Alle Zuschauer sind neugierig und gespannt. Der Anwalt setzt sich auf das **Sofa** und lässt eine Münze aus seiner Hand fallen. Die Münze fällt nach unten, bleibt aber auf halbem Weg in der Luft stehen. Die Münze bleibt in der Luft und fällt nicht herunter.

"Wow!", rufen die Kinder.

Er lässt eine weitere Münze fallen, welche ebenfalls nicht zu Boden fällt. Alle Kinder klatschen erstaunt in die Hände.

"Das ist großartig!", sagt die Lehrerin. „Wie haben Sie das gelernt?"

„Mein Onkel war Zauberer, und von ihm habe ich viele Tricks gelernt."

Die Lehrerin und der Anwalt sprechen über Magie und die Kinder beginnen, im Haus des Anwalts herumzurennen und zu spielen. Der Anwalt ist ein reicher Mann. Seine Villa ist groß und luxuriös. Es gibt schöne **Vorhänge** und große französische Fenster im Wohnzimmer. Einige der Kinder rennen zum Spielen ins Foyer. Dort gibt es ein wunderschönes Aquarium, und es gefällt ihnen, die Fische zu beobachten. Rose langweilt sich. Sie mag keine einfachen Zaubertricks. Also beschließt sie, Zeit mit den Kindern zu verbringen.

Drei Mädchen sind im Essbereich und spielen "Haus". Rose schleicht sich herein und sieht ihnen beim Spielen zu. Sie spielen eine Mutter und ihre beiden Töchter als Rollenspiel. Sie haben eine kleine **Küche** in einer Ecke, wo die Mutter kocht. Die beiden Kinder warten am **Esstisch**. Ihre Mutter will ihnen Essen geben. Das ist alles, was Rose sehen kann, und es hilft nicht, sich von ihrer Ausstellung in Berlin abzulenken. Sie wundert sich, warum Jack noch nicht mit den Tickets zurückgekehrt ist. Sie geht im Haus umher. Die **Wände** sind mit wunderschönen Gemälden geschmückt. Rose bewundert jedes einzelne. Rose mag ein **Gemälde** ganz besonders. Es ist ein großes Glasgemälde, das eine Frau mit ihrem Hund zeigt.

„Spielst du mit uns Verstecken?", fragt ein kleiner Junge Rose.

Rose ist überrascht. Sie weiß nicht, was sie sagen soll. Es ist Ewigkeiten her, seit sie das letzte Mal Kinderspiele gespielt hat.

„Du spielst nicht gerne Verstecken?", sagt der Junge.

"Nein, das ist nicht wahr. Ich habe es oft gespielt, als ich ein Kind wie du war", antwortet Rose.

„Spiel jetzt mit uns."

"OK. Komm! Lass uns spielen!"

Der Junge rennt los, um die anderen Kinder zu rufen. Sie rennen begeistert auf Rose zu und der Junge sagt:

„Wir verstecken uns im Haus und Rose zählt bis 5 und sucht uns dann. Bereit?"

"Juhu! Lasst uns anfangen", rufen die Kinder begeistert.

„Lasst uns noch etwas Besonderes machen", schlägt Rose vor. „Lasst uns ein Zeitlimit für die Suche festlegen."

"Wow! Das wird sehr spannend! Wie viel Zeit haben wir?", fragt ein Kind.

"Zehn Minuten. OK?", sagt Rose.

„Ja", sagen die Kinder begeistert.

„Ich aktiviere einen Timer auf meinem Handy und wenn es klingelt, ist eure Zeit abgelaufen!" sagt Rose.

"OK!", antworten die Kinder, und das Spiel beginnt.

Rose schließt die Augen und beginnt zu zählen: „1... 2... 3... 4... 5..."

Alle Kinder verstecken sich im Haus. Rose beginnt zu suchen.

„Wo seid ihr, Kinder?!", ruft Rose und öffnet die **Tür** eines **Schlafzimmer**s.

Sie schaut unter das **Bett** und findet niemanden. Der Raum hat schlichte Wände und keine **Möbel**, also geht Rose hinaus und betritt das Nebenzimmer. Dieses ist dunkel, ohne Fenster, und es gibt nur eine brennende Lampe. Rose findet das Zimmer ein bisschen beängstigend, aber sie sieht sich um. Auch hier sind keine Kinder. Das Haus des Anwalts hat außer diesen beiden Zimmern im Erdgeschoss nur ein Wohnzimmer, ein Esszimmer und eine **Küche**. Sie geht in die Küche und sieht einen großen **Kühlschrank**, ein Gericht im **Ofen**, eine Spülmaschine voller **Geschirr**, wie **Teller**, **Schüsseln** und **Löffel**, und eine Frau, die eine Scheibe Brot in einen **Toaster** steckt. Alle **Regale** und Lagerorte sind ohne Vorhänge, also beschließt Rose, woanders zu suchen.

„Aber im Erdgeschoss kann man nirgendwo anders suchen!", wundert sich Rose.

Sie schaut sich um, um zu sehen, ob es eine Treppe gibt, die in den ersten Stock führt, und sie findet eine in einer Ecke. Sie hat nur noch fünf Minuten, also eilt Rose die Treppe hinauf. Dort ist alles ruhig. Das erste, was sie im ersten Stock findet, ist eine Tür. Sie öffnet sie und sieht, dass es ein **Badezimmer** ist. Sie findet das Badezimmer ziemlich seltsam. Dort gibt es ein **Spülbecken**, einen **Spiegel** und einen kaputten **Fernseher**.

„Das sieht eher aus wie ein Lagerraum. Aber wo sind die Kinder?", fragt sich Rose.

Sie verlässt das Badezimmer und sieht, dass der Rest des Erdgeschosses komplett leer ist. Überall sind Spinnweben und es gibt dort keine **Beleuchtung**. In einer Ecke entdeckt sie einen **Stuhl** und einen **Schrank**. Sie öffnet den Schrank und findet zwei Kartons: In einem Karton befindet sich eine **Klimaanlage**, in dem anderen eine **Heizung**.

"Seltsam!", denkt sie.

Sie findet auch eine **Steppdecke**, ein Kissen, **Bettlaken**, **Kissenbezüge** und **Bettbezüge**.

Der Timer klingelt und Rose hat keine Zeit mehr, nach den Kindern zu suchen. Rose beschließt, aufzugeben und den Schrank zu schließen. In diesem Moment bemerkt Rose eine Tür im Schrank. Rose ist sehr überrascht, die Tür zu sehen.

„Dieses Haus ist so mysteriös. Soll ich diese Tür öffnen?", denkt sie.

"Nein. Das ist nicht mein Haus. Ich sollte sie nicht

öffnen. Aber wo sind die Kinder? Warum kommen sie nicht raus?", fragt sie sich.

Sie ist verwirrt, aber beschließt dann doch, die Tür zu öffnen. Sie dreht am Knauf, und die Tür ist verschlossen. Sie sucht noch einmal nach den Kindern. Sie durchsucht sowohl das Erdgeschoss als auch den ersten Stock, kann die Kinder aber nicht finden. Der Anwalt und die Lehrerin sind im Wohnzimmer immer noch in ein Gespräch über Magie vertieft. Rose macht sich Sorgen um die Kinder. Sie geht in die Küche und fragt die Frau dort: „Haben Sie die Kinder irgendwo in der Nähe gesehen?"

„Ich habe sie vorhin im **Foyer** und im Esszimmer spielen sehen", antwortet sie, während sie etwas auf der **Herdplatte** kocht.

„Ich habe sie damals auch gesehen, aber danach haben wir angefangen, Verstecken zu spielen. Sie sind jetzt nicht mehr im Haus", sagt Rose.

„Wo sollten sie hingehen? Sie müssen einfach hier sein. Lassen Sie mich suchen", sagt die Frau und beginnt zu suchen.

Sie durchsucht jeden Raum, aber die Kinder sind nicht zu finden. Rose ist sehr besorgt.

„Wie soll ich das der Lehrerin sagen?", fragt Rose die andere Frau.

"Machen Sie sich keine Sorgen. Gehen Sie einfach und sagen Sie es ihr. Es ist nicht Ihre Schuld", sagt die Frau.

"Nein. Ich kann nicht. Es ist meine Schuld. Alle Eltern werden mir die Schuld geben."

„Hören Sie zu, Rose. Wenn Sie der Lehrerin gleich Bescheid geben, können wir schneller mit der Suche nach den Kindern beginnen. Auch der Anwalt kann uns helfen. Also keine Sorge. Gehen Sie einfach hin und sagen Sie es ihnen", sagt die Frau.

Rose holt tief Luft und geht ins Wohnzimmer.

SUMMARY

Rose, die Lehrerin, und alle zwölf Kinder sind im Haus des Anwalts. Der Anwalt zeigt ihnen Zaubertricks und alle haben Spaß. Der Anwalt und die Lehrerin beginnen, über Magie zu sprechen, aber Rose hat kein Interesse an diesem Gespräch. Rose beschließt, mit den Kindern Verstecken zu spielen. Sie besprechen die Spielregeln, und die Kinder verstecken sich im Haus. Rose soll die Kinder suchen. Sie beginnt in der Küche, im Schlafzimmer, in den verschiedenen Teilen des Erdgeschosses und sogar im ersten Stock des Hauses nach den Kindern zu suchen. Trotz ihrer Bemühungen kann sie sie nicht finden und wird ängstlich. Sie engagiert eine Frau in der Küche, um ihr zu helfen, aber sie können die Kinder immer noch nicht finden.

WORDS TO REMEMBER

1. **Haus** - House
2. **Sofa** - Sofa
3. **Tisch** - Table
4. **Esstisch** - Dining table
5. **Teppich** - Carpet
6. **Fernseher** - Television
7. **Klimaanlage** - Air-conditioner
8. **Heizung** - Heater
9. **Spülbecken** - Kitchen sink
10. **Spiegel** - Mirror

11. **Kühlschrank** - Refrigerator
12. **Toaster** - Toaster
13. **Ofen** - Oven
14. **Schrank** - Cupboard
15. **Regale** - Shelves
16. **Vorhänge** - Curtains
17. **Beleuchtung** - Lights
18. **Wohnzimmer** - Living room
19. **Schlafzimmer** - Bedroom
20. **Foyer** - Foyer
21. **Küche** - Kitchen
22. **Badezimmer** - Bathroom
23. **Bett** - Bed
24. **Kissenbezüge** - Pillowcases
25. **Bettbezüge** - Duvet covers
26. **Bettlaken** - Bedsheets
27. **Herdplatte** - Hotplate
28. **Geschirr** - Dishes
29. **Schüsseln** - Bowls
30. **Teller** - Plates
31. **Wände** - Walls
32. **Tür** - Door
33. **Möbel** - Furniture
34. **Gemälde** - Painting
35. **Stuhl** - Chair
36. **Steppdecke** - Quilt

QUESTIONS

1. Was macht die Gruppe im Wohnzimmer?

- a. Abendessen

- b. Fernsehen
- c. Einen Zaubertrick anschauen
- d. Spielen

2. Welchen Gegenstand verwendet der Anwalt für seinen Zaubertrick?

- a. Einen Schmetterling
- b. Einen Löffel
- c. Eine Münze
- d. Einen Ring

3. Welches Spiel spielt Rose mit den Kindern?

- a. Verstecken
- b. Tennis
- c. Fußball
- d. Ludo

4. Wo sucht Rose zuerst nach den Kindern?

- a. Unter dem Bett
- b. Hinter den Vorhängen
- c. Im Badezimmer
- d. Im Schrank

5. Warum ist Rose ängstlich?

- a. Weil sie krank ist
- b. Weil sie die Kinder nicht finden kann
- c. Weil sie sich langweilt
- d. Weil sie keine Freunde hat

———

ANSWERS

1. **c.** Einen Zaubertrick anschauen
2. **c.** Eine Münze
3. **a.** Verstecken
4. **a.** Unter dem Bett
5. **b.** Weil sie die Kinder nicht finden kann

———

ENGLISH TRANSLATION

Rose, the teacher, and her twelve students are at the lawyer's house. They are all gathered around a table in the living room. Their eyes are fixed on the lawyer's hand. He is showing them a magical trick. The children are very interested in the trick.

"I will now drop these coins in my hand on the carpet. Pay attention to the coins. Keep your eyes fixed on them as they leave my hand and fall down on the carpet below." the lawyer says.

All the viewers are curious and excited. The lawyer sits down on the sofa and releases one coin from his hand. The coin moves downwards but stops in the air mid-way. The coin stays in the air and doesn't fall down.

"Wow!" the children exclaim.

He drops another coin, and that doesn't fall as well. All the children clap their hands in amazement.

"This is amazing!" says the teacher. "How did you learn this?"

"My uncle was a magician, and I learnt tricks from him."

The teacher and the lawyer start talking about magic and the children begin running around playing in the lawyer's house. The lawyer is a rich man. His mansion is large and lavish. There are beautiful curtains and large French windows in the living room. Some of the children run to the foyer to play. There is a beautiful fish tank there, and they enjoy watching the fish. Rose is bored. She doesn't enjoy easy magic tricks. So, she decides to spend her time with the children.

Three girls are in the dining area enjoying a game of playing house. Rose sneaks in and watches them play. They are role-playing a mother and her two daughters. They have a little kitchen in one corner where the mother is cooking. The two children are waiting at the dining table. Their mom is about to give them food. That's all Rose can see and it doesn't help to take her mind away from her exhibition in Berlin. She wonders why Jack hasn't returned with the tickets yet. She walks around the house. The walls are adorned with beautiful paintings. Rose admires each one of them. Rose loves one painting in particular. It is a large glass painting of a woman with her dog.

"Will you play hide and seek with us?" one little boy asks Rose.

Rose is surprised. She doesn't know what to say. It has been ages since she has played little children's games.

"You don't like playing hide and seek?" the boy says.

"No, that's not true. I played a lot of it when I was a child like you," Rose replies.

"Play with us now."

"Ok. Come on! Let's play!"

The boy runs to call all the other children. They excitedly run towards Rose and the boy says,

"We will hide around the house and Rose will start looking for us at the count of 5. Ready?"

"Yay! Let's begin." all the other children yell excitedly.

"Let's add a twist to the game," Rose suggests. "Let's add a time limit to the search."

"Wow! That will be very interesting! How much time will we have?" one child asks.

"Ten minutes. Ok?" Rose says.

"Yes," the children cry out excitedly.

"I'll put a timer on my phone and when it rings, your time is up!" says Rose.

"Ok!" they reply and the game begins.

Rose closes her eyes and starts counting, "1... 2... 3... 4... 5..."

All the children hide around the house. Rose starts searching.

"Where are you children?!" exclaims Rose and opens the door of one bedroom.

She looks under the bed and finds no one. The room has plain walls and no furniture, so Rose walks out and enters the door next to it. This one is dark without any windows, and there is just one burning lamp. Rose finds the room a bit scary but she looks around it. There are no children here either. The lawyer's house only has a living room, dining room, and a kitchen other than these two rooms on the ground floor. She walks into the kitchen and finds a large refrigerator, something cooking in the oven, a dishwasher full of dishes, like plates, bowls, and spoons, and a woman placing a slice of bread inside a toaster. All the shelves and storage areas are without shutters, so Rose decides to search elsewhere.

"But there is nowhere else to search on the ground floor!" Rose wonders.

She looks around to see if there is a flight of stairs leading to the first floor, and she finds one in a corner. There are only five minutes left on the clock, so Rose rushes up the stairs. Everything is quiet there. The first thing she finds on the first floor is a door. She opens it, and it is a bathroom. She finds the bathroom to be quite weird. There is a kitchen sink there, a mirror, and a broken television.

"This seems more like a storeroom. But where are the children?" Rose thinks to herself.

She walks out of the bathroom and sees that the rest of the first floor is completely empty. There are spiderwebs everywhere and there are no lights there. She spots a chair and a cupboard in one corner. She opens the cupboard and finds two carton boxes: in one box there is an air conditioner and in the other a heater.

"Strange!" she thinks.

She also finds a quilt, a cushion, bedsheets, pillowcases, and duvet covers.

The timer rings and Rose has no time to search for the children. Rose decides to give up and close the cupboard. Just then, Rose notices a door inside the cupboard. Rose is very surprised to see the door.

"This house is so mysterious. Shall I open this door?" she thinks.

"No. This is not my house. I should not open it. But where are the children? Why are they not coming out?" she wonders.

She is confused, but she finally decides to open the door. She turns the knob, and the door is locked. She looks for the children once again. She searches both the ground floor as well as the first floor, but she cannot find the children. The lawyer and the teacher are still deep in conversation about magic in the living room. Rose is worried about the children. She walks to the kitchen and asks the woman there, "Did you see the children anywhere around?"

"I saw them playing in the foyer and the dining room a little while ago," she replies while cooking something on the hotplate.

"I also saw them at that time, but after that, we started playing hide and seek. They are not in the house now," Rose says.

"Where can they go? They must be just here. Let me search," the woman says and starts looking.

She searches every room, but the children are not to be found. Rose is very anxious.

"How will I let the teacher know?" Rose asks this other woman.

"Don't worry. Just go and tell her. It is not your fault," the woman says.

"No. I cannot. It is my fault. All the parents will blame me."

"Listen, Rose. If you tell the teacher right away, we can start looking for the children faster. The lawyer can also help us. So, don't worry. Just go and tell them," says the woman.

Rose takes a deep breath and walks towards the living room.

4
THE SEARCH
QUESTION WORDS

Rose geht langsam ins Wohnzimmer. Sie weiß nicht, **wie** sie anfangen soll. Die Lehrerin und der Anwalt sitzen auf dem Sofa. Sie genießen ihre Unterhaltung. Rose sitzt auf einem Stuhl neben der Lehrerin.

„Wir reden über Magie. Er erzählt mir von seinen Lebenserfahrungen mit Magie. Das ist wirklich faszinierend", sagt die Lehrerin.

Rose bringt ein Lächeln zustande.

"**Wo** sind die Kinder? Lassen Sie mich sie mit ein paar weiteren spannenden Tricks unterhalten!", sagt der Anwalt.

"Oh ja! Das wird den Kindern wirklich gefallen! Sie sollten auch zu uns in die Schule kommen, damit andere Kinder sich an Ihrer Magie erfreuen können!", sagt die Lehrerin.

„Jetzt noch nicht. Sobald ich in Rente bin, melde ich mich bei Ihnen", sagt der Anwalt lachend.

Auch die Lehrerin lacht. Rose ist sehr verzweifelt. Sie hat nicht den Mut, der Lehrerin von den Kindern zu erzählen.

„**Wie viele** Kinder haben Sie an Ihrer Schule?", fragt der Anwalt.

„Wir haben fünfzig Studenten. Ich bin für die zwölf Vorschulkinder hier verantwortlich. Es gibt drei andere Lehrer, die sich um den Rest kümmern."

"Und **wie viel** verdienen Sie?", fragt der Anwalt.

„Nun, viel weniger als du. Ich verdiene gerade genug, um mich und meine Mutter zu ernähren. Wir führen ein einfaches Leben."

„Wahres Glück liegt in den einfachen Dingen des Lebens. **Wie lange** unterrichten Sie schon?"

„Lassen Sie mich überlegen, **wann** ich angefangen habe. Ich habe mit zweiundzwanzig angefangen und bin jetzt fünfzig. Es sind also gute achtundzwanzig Jahre vergangen. Ich unterrichte sehr gerne und bin gerne mit Kindern zusammen", sagt die Lehrerin.

"Oh! Sie sind fünfzig Jahre alt? Sie sehen ziemlich jung aus!"

"Vielen Dank. Das ist ein wunderbares Kompliment. **Wie alt** sind Sie?", fragt die Lehrerin lächelnd.

"Können Sie raten?", sagt der Anwalt.

„Ähm… Ungefähr fünfundvierzig?«

"Perfekt! Ich bin fünfundvierzig." sagt der Anwalt.

Die Lehrerin und der Anwalt lachen.

„**Wie kommt es**, dass die Kinder heute so still sind?", bemerkt die Lehrerin und sieht sich um.

Rose wird rot. Sie beginnt zu schwitzen.

„Warum sehen Sie so aufgebracht aus? Was ist passiert? Sie sehen besorgt aus", fragt der Anwalt Rose.

„Ähm, nichts. Mir geht es gut. Eigentlich möchte ich Ihnen beiden etwas sagen", sagt Rose.

"Ja, bitte. Schießen Sie los", sagt der Anwalt.

„Vor einiger Zeit habe ich mit den Kindern Verstecken gespielt. Ich war dran mit Suchen, und ich sagte den

Kindern, sie sollten sich verstecken. Ich habe das ganze Haus durchsucht, aber die Kinder sind nicht zu finden. Oh, es tut mir sehr leid ", sagt Rose mit Tränen in den Augen.

"Du meine Güte! Haben Sie überall im Haus gesucht? ", sagt die Lehrerin alarmiert.

„Ja, das habe ich, zweimal. Ich weiß nicht, wo sie sind", sagt Rose.

„Ich werde Ärger bekommen. Wo können alle zwölf von ihnen hin?!", sagt die Lehrerin, als sie anfängt, im Haus nach den Kindern zu suchen.

Rose begleitet die Lehrerin bei der Suche, während der Anwalt im Wohnzimmer bleibt und nachdenkt. Nach ungefähr 15 Minuten kommt die Lehrerin zurück ins Wohnzimmer.

„Ich brauche Ihre Hilfe", fleht sie den Anwalt an. „Ich kann die Kinder nicht finden. Bitte helfen Sie mir."

„Haben Sie außerhalb des Hauses gesucht? Vielleicht spielen sie auf der Straße", sagt der Anwalt.

„Nein, habe ich nicht. Aber ich hatte sie angewiesen, drinnen zu bleiben. Sie gehen selten gegen meine Anweisungen", sagt die Lehrerin.

„Vielleicht ist heute dieser seltene Anlass", sagt der Anwalt.

„Er hat Recht", sagt Rose.

Die Lehrerin stimmt zu und alle gehen auf die Straße, um zu suchen. Auch der Anwalt begleitet sie. Draußen ist alles ruhig. Die Straße ist völlig leer. Die Lehrerin geht den Hügel auf und ab und ruft die Namen aller Kinder. „Tom! Ted! Johnny! Lizzy! Komm raus, bitte. Spielt nicht den Narren, Kinder! Hört auf mit dem Unfug!"

Es kommt keine Antwort. Auch Rose fleht die Kinder an: „Bitte kommt heraus! Wir alle suchen euch!"

Der Anwalt steht auf der Straße und beobachtet die

Szene. Er sieht sich in alle Richtungen um, sagt aber nichts.

„Die Kinder sind nicht auf der Straße", sagt der Anwalt.

Die Lehrerin und Rose sind überrascht, das zu hören.

"**Warum** sagen Sie das? Wo sind die Kinder dann?", fragt die Lehrerin.

"Sie sind im Haus", antwortet der Anwalt.

„Aber wir haben gerade das ganze Haus durchsucht. Die Kinder sind sicher nicht drin", sagt die Lehrerin.

„Sie sind nicht in meinem Haus."

„In **welchem** Haus sind sie?", fragt Rose.

„Das erste Haus der Straße."

"**Wessen** Haus ist das? Und woher wissen Sie, dass die Kinder da sind?", sagt die Lehrerin.

„Weil ich Anwalt bin."

„Oh ja, auf jeden Fall. Aber warum sollten die Kinder mitten in einem Versteckspiel dorthin gehen?", fragt Rose.

"Beantworten Sie meine Frage. **Wie weit** weg ist das Haus von hier?", fragt der Anwalt.

„Vielleicht fünf Minuten. Aber warum fragen Sie?", sagt die Lehrerin.

„Wann haben Sie die Kinder zuletzt gesehen? Und **wer**, glauben Sie, hat sie zuletzt gesehen?", fragt der Anwalt Rose.

„Ich habe sie vor dem Spiel gesehen. Aber ich weiß nicht, ob sie nach mir noch jemand gesehen hat."

„Mit **wem** haben sie zuletzt gesprochen?"

„Ich glaube, sie haben zuletzt mit mir gesprochen", sagt Rose. Sie hat große Angst. „Aber ich habe nichts getan. Ich weiß nicht, wer sie mitgenommen hat."

„Das bedeutet, dass sich die Kinder überhaupt nicht versteckt haben. Kaum hatten Sie die Augen geschlossen, rannten sie aus dem Haus. Tatsächlich wollten sie, dass Sie

Ihre Augen schließen, weil Sie auf die Kinder aufgepasst haben."

"Wozu?" sagt Rose.

„Sie müssen in Gefahr sein! Lassen Sie uns gehen und sie retten, wenn Sie sicher sind, dass sie in diesem Haus sind", sagt die besorgte Lehrerin.

„Sie sind nicht in Gefahr", sagt der Anwalt.

"Was?", fragt Rose.

„Dieses Haus gehört mir. Die Kinder und ich haben euch beiden einen Streich gespielt", sagt der Anwalt lachend.

"Das ist nicht fair! Sie haben mich zu Tode erschreckt", sagt die Lehrerin.

Alle lachen.

SUMMARY

Rose will der Lehrerin von den vermissten Kindern erzählen, also gesellt sie sich zu dem Anwalt und der Lehrerin ins Wohnzimmer. Sie lauscht ihrem Gespräch, bringt aber nicht genug Mut auf, ihnen die Neuigkeit zu überbringen. Schließlich überbringt sie dem Anwalt und der Lehrerin die Neuigkeit und sie beginnen alle, nach den Kindern zu suchen. Die Lehrerin ist sehr ängstlich und besorgt. Nervös suchen sie im Haus und auch auf der Straße nach den Kindern. Der Anwalt versucht, ihnen noch mehr Angst zu machen und enthüllt schließlich, dass die Kinder in Sicherheit sind und dass dies ein Streich war, den er mit ihnen geplant hat.

WORDS TO REMEMBER

1. **Was** - What
2. **Wo** - Where
3. **Wann** - When
4. **Warum** - Why
5. **Wer** - Who
6. **Wem** - Whom
7. **Wie kommt es** - How come
8. **Wie** - How
9. **welches** - Which
10. **Wessen** - Whose
11. **Wie viel** - How much
12. **Wie viele** - How many
13. **Wozu** - What for
14. **Wie lange** - How long
15. **Wie alt** - How old
16. **Wie weit** - How far

QUESTIONS

1. Wie alt ist der Rechtsanwalt?

- a. Er ist 35 Jahre alt
- b. Er ist 40 Jahre alt
- c. Er ist 45 Jahre alt
- d. Er ist 50 Jahre alt

2. Wo sitzt Rose im Wohnzimmer?

- a. Auf dem Sofa
- b. Auf dem Stuhl
- c. Auf der Couch
- d. Auf dem Hocker

3. Was macht der Anwalt, als die Lehrerin ihn einlädt, seine Zaubertricks an ihrer Schule zu zeigen?

- a. Er nimmt die Einladung an
- b. Er wird wütend
- c. Er beleidigt die Lehrerin
- d. Höflich sagt er, dass er dies tun werde, wenn er in Rente ist

4. Wo schlägt der Anwalt vor, nach den Kindern zu suchen?

- a. In der Küche
- b. Im Park
- c. Auf der Straße
- d. In der Garage

5. Wo verstecken sich die Kinder?

- a. Im Schrank
- b. Im zweiten Haus des Anwalts
- c. Auf der Terrasse

- d. Niemand weiß es

ANSWERS

1. **c.** Er ist 45 Jahre alt
2. **b.** Auf dem Stuhl
3. **d.** Höflich sagt er, dass er dies tun werde, wenn er in Rente ist
4. **c.** Auf der Straße
5. **b.** Im zweiten Haus des Anwalts

ENGLISH TRANSLATION

Rose slowly walks into the living room. She doesn't know how to start. The teacher and the lawyer are seated on the sofa. They are enjoying their conversation. Rose sits on a chair next to the teacher.

"We are talking about magic. He is telling me about his real-life experiences with magic. It's really fascinating," the teacher says.

Rose manages a smile.

"Where are the children? Let me entertain them with a few more exciting tricks!" says the lawyer.

"Oh yes! The children will really enjoy it! You should also come over to our school so that other children can enjoy your magic!" the teacher says.

"Not just yet, madam. I will contact you once I retire," the lawyer says, laughing.

The teacher also laughs. Rose is very distressed. She

doesn't have the courage to tell the teacher about the children.

"How many children do you have in your school?" the lawyer asks.

"There are fifty students. I am in charge of the twelve students here. There are three other teachers to take care of the remaining."

"And how much do you make?" the lawyer asks.

"Well, much less than you do. I make just enough to support myself and my mother. We live a simple life."

"Real happiness is in the simple things of life, madam. How long have you been teaching?"

"I started when I was twenty-two and I am fifty now. So it's been a good twenty-eight years. I love teaching and I enjoy spending time with children," says the teacher.

"Oh! You are fifty years old? You look quite young!"

"Thank you. That's a wonderful compliment. How old are you?" the teacher says smiling.

"Can you make a guess?" says the lawyer.

"Uhm. Around forty-five?"

"Perfect! I am forty-five." the lawyer says.

The teacher and the lawyer laugh.

"How come the children are so quiet today?" the teacher remarks looking around.

Rose's face turns red. She begins to sweat.

"Why are you looking so upset? What happened? You look worried," the lawyer asks Rose.

"Uhm, nothing. I am fine. Actually, there is something I want to tell you both," Rose says.

"Yes, please. Go ahead," the lawyer says.

"I was playing hide and seek with the children a little while ago. I was the seeker in the game, and I told the children to hide. I have searched the entire house but the children are not to be found. Oh, I am very sorry about this, madam," Rose says teary-eyed.

"Oh, my goodness! Did you search everywhere in the house?" says the teacher, alarmed.

"Yes, I did twice. I don't know where they are," says Rose.

"I am going to get in trouble. Where can all the twelve of them go?!" the teacher says as she starts looking for the children around the house.

Rose joins the teacher in the search, while the lawyer remains in the living room, thinking. After about fifteen minutes, the teacher comes back to the living room.

"I need your help, sir," she pleads with the lawyer. "I am unable to find the children. Please help me."

"Did you search outside the house? They might be playing on the street." the lawyer says.

"No, I didn't. But I had instructed them to stay inside. They rarely go against my instructions," says the teacher.

"Maybe today is that rare occasion," the lawyer says.

"He is correct," Rose says.

The teacher agrees and they all go out to the street to search. The lawyer also accompanies them. Everything outside is quiet. The street is totally empty. The teacher goes up and down the hill calling out the names of all the children. "Tom! Ted! Johnny! Lizzy! Come out, please. Don't play the fool, children! Stop your mischief!"

There is no answer. Rose also pleads with the children, "Please come out! We are all looking for you!"

The lawyer stands on the street, taking in the scene. He looks around in all directions but says nothing.

"The children are not on the street." The lawyer says.

The teacher and Rose are surprised to hear this.

"Why do you say this? Where are the children then?" asks the teacher.

"They are in the house." the lawyer replies.

"But we just searched the entire house. The children are surely not inside." the teacher says.

"They are not in my house."

"In which house are they?" Rose asks.

"The first house on the street."

"Whose house is that? And how do you know the children are there?" says the teacher.

"Because I am a lawyer."

"Oh yes definitely. But why would the children go there in the middle of a game of hide and seek?" Rose asks.

"Answer my question. How far is that house from here? " the lawyer asks.

"Maybe five minutes. But why are you asking?" says the teacher.

"When did you see the children last? And who do you think saw them last?" the lawyer asks Rose.

"I saw them before the game. But I don't know if anyone else saw them after me."

"To whom did they speak to last?"

"I think they spoke to me last," Rose says. She is very afraid. "But I didn't do anything. I don't know who took them away."

"This means that the children didn't hide at all. As soon as you closed your eyes, they ran out of the house. In fact, they wanted you to close your eyes because you were keeping a watch on them."

"What for?" says Rose.

"They must be in danger! Let's go and rescue them if you are sure that they are in that house." the worried teacher says.

"They are not in danger," the lawyer says.

"What?" Rose asks.

"That house is mine. The children and I played a prank on you both," the lawyer says, laughing.

"This is not fair! You scared me to death," the teacher says.

All of them laugh.

5
THE WEEKEND
LIKES & DISLIKES

Das Abenteuer der vermissten Kinder ist vorbei. Die Lehrerin ist mit den Kindern in der Garage des Anwalts. Der Anwalt schläft in seinem Zimmer. Rose ist an einem warmen Freitagnachmittag auf der Straße und genießt die Sonne. Rose **liebt** die Sonne, aber ihre Augen sind auf den Bildschirm ihres Handys gerichtet.

„Hallo Rose. Die Geschäftsführung hat einen weiteren Vertreter des Unternehmens zur Betreuung der Ausstellung entsandt. Sie können zum frühestmöglichen Zeitpunkt nach Florenz zurückkehren. Bitte kommen Sie nicht zur Ausstellung nach Deutschland. Vielen Dank."

Das ist die Nachricht auf ihrem Bildschirm. Rose ist sehr enttäuscht. **Sie hasst** das italienische Schienensystem. Sie fühlt sich unsicher in Bezug auf ihren Arbeitsplatz im Unternehmen.

"Hallo Rose!", ruft ihr eine Stimme von hinten zu.

Sie schließt die Nachricht in ihrem Handy und dreht sich um, um zu sehen, wer es ist. Es ist Jack. Rose freut sich sehr, ihn zu sehen. Sie **mag** es, mit ihm zusammen zu sein; also freut sie sich, dass er zurück ist.

"Hi! Was für eine Überraschung! Endlich bist du zurück. Ich freue mich, dich zu sehen", sagt sie ihm.

Jack lächelt und sagt: „Ich habe Tickets nach Berlin für uns alle. Für dich, mich, die Lehrerin und alle Kinder. Wir müssen in einer Stunde zum Flughafen aufbrechen. Der Flughafen ist zwei Stunden von diesem Dorf entfernt. Ich habe zwei Taxis für die Fahrt bestellt. Sie werden gleich hier sein."

Rose sagt nichts. Sie sieht nicht begeistert aus.

"Was ist los? Bist du nicht froh, dass du es rechtzeitig schaffen wirst?", fragt Jack.

„Meine Firma hat jemand anderen geschickt, um die Ausstellung in Berlin zu betreuen. Sie haben mir gesagt, ich solle nach Florenz zurückkommen. Also glaube ich nicht, dass ich mich dir anschließen kann", sagt Rose.

"Oh..."

"Ja. Ich habe gerade eine Nachricht von meinem Kollegen erhalten. Es tut mir leid wegen der Mühe. Ich bezahle dir mein Ticket."

"Keine Bange! Was hast du jetzt vor?"

„Ich habe noch gar nichts geplant."

„Von diesem Flughafen aus gibt es keinen Direktflug nach Florenz", sagt Jack.

"Lass mich sehen was ich machen kann. Morgen ist Samstag, also kann ich mir Zeit nehmen, um Florenz zu erreichen. Ich muss erst am Montag zur Arbeit,", sagt Rose.

"Ja. Auch ich habe meine Meetings auf Montag verschoben. Bis ich heute Abend in Berlin lande, wird es schon spät sein. Es wäre also nicht fair gegenüber dem Kunden", erklärt Jack.

„Gibt es tagsüber keinen Flug nach Berlin?"

"Leider nicht."

„Also haben wir am Wochenende alle frei", bemerkt Rose.

"Ja", sagt Jack lächelnd.

"Du hast Glück. Du kannst dein Wochenende auf deutsche Art genießen", sagt Rose.

„Ja, aber **ich bevorzuge es nicht**, alleine Urlaub zu machen."

„Oh, ich bin das genaue Gegenteil. **Es macht mir nichts aus**, alleine zu reisen. Ich lege mehr Wert auf das Reiseziel als auf die Menschen", sagt Rose.

„**Ich bevorzuge** erholsame Ferien. Zeit am Strand und im Pool zu verbringen und den Sand und die Wellen zu genießen, sind meine Lieblingsbeschäftigungen."

„**Ich würde lieber** meinen Tag im Museum verbringen, Kunstwerke bewundern und etwas über Geschichte und Kultur lernen. **Ich verabscheue es**, untätig zu sein", sagt Rose.

Jack lacht. „Du bist wirklich das genaue Gegenteil von mir", sagt er.

„**Ich will** alleine nach Afrika reisen", sagt Rose begeistert.

„Was **möchtest du** dort sehen?"

„**Ich bestaune** die Tierwelt! Ich könnte den ganzen Tag damit verbringen, Tiere und Vögel zu beobachten!"

Jack lächelt. „Wieder Gegensätze!"

"Warum? **Magst du nicht** die Tierwelt?", fragt Rose.

„**Ich kann** Tiere **nicht ausstehen**. Als ich noch sehr jung war, wurde ich von einer Schlange angegriffen, und auch meine Erfahrungen mit Haustieren waren nicht so toll", sagt Jack.

„Du solltest einmal eine Wanderung im Amazonas-Regenwald machen. Ich bin sicher, du wirst dich in die wilden Tiere verlieben."

"**Niemals**! **Ich kann** den Geruch von Tieren **nicht** einmal für eine Minute **tolerieren**."

„**Ich bin verrückt nach** Affen und Papageien. Oh, ich liebe sie so sehr! Was ist die eine Sache im Leben, **in die du vernarrt bist**?", fragt Rose.

„Ähm… Das Meer und meine Freundin", sagt Jack.

„**Ich kann** das Gefühl von Sand auf meiner Haut **nicht ertragen**. Aber ich möchte auch vernarrt in einen Freund sein", sagt Rose.

„Verliebt sein ist schön!", ruft Jack.

„Ich liebe das Gefühl, verliebt zu sein! Ich hoffe, ich kann es bald erleben", sagt Rose.

„Warst du noch nie verliebt?"

"Nein. **Gar nicht**!"

„Ich bin mir sicher, dass du es bald sein wirst. Und wenn du es bist, wirst du anfangen, das Meer zu lieben", sagt Jack.

„Wo hast du deine Freundin kennengelernt? Am Strand?"

"**Genau**! Wie hast du das erraten?"

Rose lächelt und sagt: „Deine Liebe leuchtet in deinen Augen."

Jack lächelt.

„Wäre es nicht ein Spaß, zusammen in den Urlaub zu fahren? Jetzt, wo wir Freunde sind, denke ich, **wir sollten** das tun."

„Spaß oder nicht, ich weiß es nicht, aber es wird sicher ein Abenteuer", sagt Jack.

Beide lachen.

„Ich habe eine tolle Idee!", sagt Rose.

"Was?"

„Lass uns dieses Wochenende zu einem Abenteuer machen! Da wir beide frei haben, lass uns ein bisschen Spaß haben!", sagt Rose.

"Ja! Gute Idee!", sagt Jack.

Rose ist begeistert und öffnet eine Karte auf ihrem Handy.

SUMMARY

Rose erhält eine Nachricht von ihrer Firma, dass jemand anderes aus ihrem Büro ausgewählt wurde, um an der Ausstellung teilzunehmen. Sie ist verärgert. Jack kommt und sie erzählt ihm davon. Jack erzählt ihr von der Änderung seines Terminplans. Sie besprechen ihre Reisevorlieben und beschließen, das Wochenende zusammen zu verbringen.

WORDS TO REMEMBER

1. **Mögen** – To like
2. **Nicht mögen** - Dislike
3. **ich bestaune** - I marvel at
4. **Ich verabscheue** - I detest
5. **ich bevorzuge** - I prefer
6. **Ich bevorzuge es nicht** - I don't prefer
7. **Ich kann ..... nicht ausstehen** - I can't stand
8. **Es macht mir nichts aus** - I don't mind
9. **Ich kann ..... nicht tolerieren** - I cannot tolerate
10. **Ich will** - I want
11. **Möchtest du** - Would you like

12. **Ich kann es nicht ertragen** - I can't bear
13. **Genau** - Exactly
14. **Gar nicht** - Not at all
15. **Niemals** - Never
16. **Du bist vernarrt in .....** - You're mad after
17. **Ich bin verrückt nach .....** - I am crazy after
18. **Liebt** - Loves
19. **Sie hasst** - She hates
20. **Ich würde lieber** - I would rather
21. **Wir sollten** - We should

QUESTIONS

1. Was teilt Roses Kollege ihr per Nachricht mit?

- a. Dass die Ausstellung abgesagt wird
- b. Dass die Ausstellung verschoben wird
- c. Dass Rose gefeuert wurde
- d. Dass Rose für die Ausstellung nicht nach Berlin reisen muss

2. Was macht Jack mit seinen Meetings?

- a. Er verschiebt sie auf Montag
- b. Er sagt sie ab
- c. Er verschiebt sie um ein paar Stunden
- d. Er verschiebt sie auf Freitag

3. Was verabscheut Rose?

- a. Im Urlaub untätig zu sein
- b. Besuch des Museums im Urlaub
- c. Im Urlaub die über Geschichte des Urlaubsortes zu lernen
- d. Im Urlaub über die Kultur des Urlaubsortes zu lernen

4. Welche der folgenden Aussagen ist richtig?

- a. Rose und Jack sind die gleiche Art von Menschen
- b. Rose und Jack sind gegensätzlich
- c. Rose und Jack sind Feinde
- d. Rose ist Jacks Freundin

5. Was wollen Rose und Jack gemeinsam verbringen?

- a. Die Sommerferien
- b. Weihnachten
- c. Das Wochenende
- d. Montagabend

ANSWERS

1. **d.** Dass Rose für die Ausstellung nicht nach Berlin reisen muss

2. **a.** Er verschiebt sie auf Montag
3. **a.** Im Urlaub untätig zu sein
4. **a.** Rose und Jack sind gegensätzlich
5. **c.** Das Wochenende

ENGLISH TRANSLATION

The adventure of the missing children is over. The teacher is in the lawyer's garage with the children. The lawyer is asleep in his room. Rose is on the street enjoying the sunshine on a warm Friday afternoon. Rose loves the sun but her eyes are on her mobile phone's screen.

"Hi, Rose. The management has sent another representative from the company to take care of the exhibition. You can return back to Florence at the earliest available opportunity. Please do not come to Germany for the exhibition. Thank you."

This is the message on her screen. Rose is very disappointed. She hates the Italian rail system. She feels insecure about her job in the company.

"Hello, Rose!" a voice calls out to her from behind.

She shuts the message in her phone and turns around to see who it is. It's Jack. Rose is extremely happy to see him. She likes his company, so she is delighted that he is back.

"Hi! What a surprise! Finally, you're back. I'm glad to see you," she tells him.

Jack smiles and says, "I have tickets to Berlin for all of us. You, me, the teacher and all the children. We will have to leave for the airport in an hour. The airport is a two-hour drive from this village. I have arranged two cabs for the journey. They will be here in a while."

Rose says nothing. She doesn't look excited.

"What's the matter? Are you not happy you're going to make it?" Jack asks.

"My company has sent someone else to handle the exhibition in Berlin. They have told me to return to Florence. So I don't think I can join you." says Rose.

"Oh… "

"Yes. I just received a message from my colleague. I am sorry about the trouble. I will pay you for my ticket."

"No worries! So what do you plan to do now?"

"I haven't planned anything yet."

"There is no direct flight to Florence from this airport," Jack says.

"Let me see what I can do. Tomorrow is Saturday, so I can take my time to reach Florence. I have to go to work only on Monday." Rose says.

"Yes. I too have postponed my meetings to Monday. It will be late by the time I land in Berlin tonight. So, it wouldn't be fair for the client." Jack explains.

"Isn't there a flight to Berlin during the day?"

"Unfortunately, no."

"So we're all free during the weekend," Rose remarks.

"Yes." Jack says smiling.

"You are so lucky. You can enjoy your weekend the German way." Rose says.

"Yeah, but I don't prefer holidaying alone."

"Oh, I am the opposite. I don't mind traveling alone. I am more particular about the destination than the people," Rose says.

"I prefer relaxing holidays. Spending time on the beach, in the pool, and enjoying the sand and the waves are my favorite activities."

"I would rather spend my day in the museum admiring

art pieces and learning about history and culture. I detest being idle," Rose says.

Jack laughs. "You are truly my polar opposite," he says.

"I want to go on a solo trip to Africa," Rose says excitedly.

"What would you like to see there?"

"I adore wildlife! I can spend all day watching animals and birds!"

Jack smiles. "Opposites again!"

"Why? Do you dislike wildlife?" Rose asks.

"I can't stand animals. I was attacked by a snake when I was very young, and my experiences with pets haven't been great too." Jack says.

"You should go on a trek in the Amazon rainforest once. I am sure you will fall in love with everything wild."

"Never! I cannot tolerate the smell of animals even for a minute."

"I am crazy about monkeys and parrots. Oh, I love them so much! What's the one thing in life you are mad about?" Rose asks.

"Uhm… The sea and my girlfriend," Jack says.

"I can't bear the feeling of sand on my skin. But I too want to be crazy about a boyfriend," Rose says.

"Being in love is beautiful!" Jack exclaims.

"I love the feeling of being in love! I hope I get to experience it soon." Rose says.

"Haven't you been in love ever?"

"No. Not at all!"

"I am certain you will very soon. And when you do, you will start loving the sea." Jack says.

"Where did you meet your girlfriend? On the beach?"

"Very much! How did you guess?"

Rose smiles and says, "Your love shines in your eyes."

Jack smiles.

"Wouldn't it be fun to go on a holiday together? Now that we are friends, I think we should."

"Fun or not I don't know, but it will surely be an adventure," Jack says.

Both of them laugh.

"I have an amazing idea!" Rose says.

"What?"

"Let's make this weekend that adventure! Since both of us are free, let's have some fun!" Rose says.

"Well, yeah! Good idea!" Jack says.

Rose is excited and opens a map on her phone.

6
THE ADVENTURE
PREPOSITIONS + TO BE/TO HAVE

Sowohl Jack als auch Rose sehen sich die Karte **von** Italien und den Ländern **um** Italien **herum** an. Es gibt so viele Orte. Sie sind verwirrt. Sie sind nicht in der Lage, sich **zu** entscheiden, welcher **unter** den verschiedenen Orten der richtige für sie ist.

„Ich denke, es ist keine gute Idee, diese Karte zur Auswahl eines Reiseziels zu verwenden", sagt Rose.

"Ich stimme zu. Was machen wir dann?", sagt Jack.

„Ich glaube nicht, dass es hier ein Reisebüro gibt, das uns helfen kann."

"Es gibt eins."

"Wo ist es? Hast du ihre Adresse?", fragt Rose.

"Ja! **Er ist** Herr Google. Und er lebt genau hier, **in** meiner Tasche", scherzt Jack.

Rose lacht. **Sie ist** amüsiert. Jack öffnet sein Handy und beginnt zu surfen.

„**Wir haben** also zwei Tage Zeit. Möchtest du einen eintägigen oder einen zweitägigen Ausflug machen?", fragt Jack.

„Da wir beide nach Florenz reisen müssen, können wir einen Ausflug in die Nähe der Stadt unternehmen.

Nachdem wir den Samstag und den halben Sonntag **an** unserem gewählten Reiseziel verbracht haben, können wir **von** dort direkt nach Florenz reisen. Was denkst du?"

"Großartige Idee!", sagt Jack.

„**Ich bin** ein abenteuerlustiger Mensch. Ich liebe Überraschungen! Also lass uns das tun. Du planst die Reise, aber sagst mir jetzt noch nichts. Das wird ein riesiger Spaß!", sagt Rose.

„Bist du sicher, dass du dich auf meine Entscheidung verlassen willst? Wir kennen uns kaum."

„Ich bin mir vollkommen sicher. Wir kennen uns nicht gut, aber **wir sind** auch keine Fremden."

"Also gut! Ich werde das tun."

„Aber bitte plane keine Zug- und Flugreisen. Wir wollen keine Verzögerungen und Zwischenstopps mehr. Mein Chef wird mich sicher feuern, wenn ich am Montagmorgen nicht zur Arbeit komme", sagt Rose.

"Erledigt! Mach dich bereit für das Abenteuer!", sagt Jack **mit** einem Augenzwinkern.

Rose ist gespannt, wohin Jack sie bringen wird.

„**Bevor** ich mit der Buchung beginne, sollten wir die Lehrerin und die Kinder fragen, ob sie uns **auf** dieser Reise begleiten möchten."

„Ähm... ich denke schon, ja. Aber ich denke, sie werden nicht mitkommen wollen. Die Lehrerin hat einen Zeitplan, an den sie sich halten muss", sagt Rose. Sie will sie nicht auf dieser Reise dabeihaben.

„Lass mich nur einmal die Lehrerin fragen", sagt Jack und geht **auf** die Garage **zu**. Rose setzt sich auf einen großen Stein **unter** einem Baum und wartet auf seine Rückkehr. **Sie hat** jetzt Gefühle für Jack. Sie sieht ihm nach, als er **neben** der Reihe der Erdbeerpflanzen **in** die Garage geht. Sie träumt von der Reise, während sie auf die schönen Zweige **über** sich blickt, die im Wind tanzen.

„**Er ist** so charmant!", denkt sie sich.

Nach ungefähr 10 Minuten kommt Jack mit der Lehrerin **aus** der Garage **heraus**. Alle zwölf Kinder folgen ihnen und **sie haben** ihre Taschen in der Hand. Sie sieht die Lehrerin an und lächelt, aber **in** ihrem Herzen ist sie nicht glücklich, weil sie weiß, dass die Lehrerin und die Kinder mitkommen werden.

„Packe deine Koffer, Rose! Wir werden in 30 Minuten aufbrechen. Wir müssen unser Ziel vor Einbruch der Dunkelheit erreichen", sagt Jack zu ihr.

"Oh ja! Ich bin so aufgeregt! Ich werde bereit sein."

Sie geht **weg**, **vorbei an** der Gruppe ins Haus des Anwalts, um ihre Taschen zu holen. Sie zieht schnell ihre Tasche **unter** dem Tisch hervor und legt ihre Sachen **hinein**. Dann fährt sie mit einem Kamm **durch** ihr glänzendes schwarzes Haar und tritt mit ihren Taschen aus dem Haus. Sie sieht ein leeres wartendes Auto und einen Kleinbus, in dem die Kinder mit ihrer Lehrerin sitzen. Sie sieht in die unschuldigen Gesichter der Kinder und ist traurig. Sie erkennt, dass sie egoistisch war. Sie möchte nun, dass sie auf die Reise mitkommen. Die Lehrerin springt aus dem Kleinbus und kommt auf Rose zu gerannt.

Sie legt Roses Hand **zwischen** ihre Hände und sagt: „Es war wirklich ein Vergnügen, Sie kennenzulernen und Zeit mit Ihnen zu verbringen. Ich hoffe, Sie einmal wieder zu sehen."

„Sind Sie und die Kinder nicht auf unserer Reise mit dabei?", fragt Rose überrascht.

„Nein, Liebes. **Wir müssen** gehen."

"**Ich habe** eine Idee! Warum kommen Sie nicht für einen Tag mit uns und reisen dann ab? **Sie haben** zwei Tage Zeit, bevor die Schulwoche beginnt. Ich denke, Jack hat mit Ihnen über die Reise gesprochen, richtig? **Er hat** etwas wirklich Aufregendes geplant!"

„Die Schule und die Eltern der Kinder wollen, dass wir sofort zurückkehren. **Sie sind** besorgt um die Kleinen", sagt die Lehrerin.

Rose umarmt die Lehrerin und die Kinder. Auch der Anwalt und Jack verabschieden sich von ihnen. Der Kleinbus mit der Lehrerin und ihren Vorschulkindern rast davon. Jack und Rose danken auch dem Anwalt für seine Freundlichkeit und Gastfreundschaft. Sie laden ihre Taschen in das wartende Auto und fahren los. Der Anwalt sieht zu, wie das Auto bergab fährt und in der Ferne verschwindet.

SUMMARY

Jack und Rose planen einen Wochenendausflug. Rose sagt, dass sie Überraschungen und Abenteuer mag und bittet Jack, die Reise zu planen, ohne ihr etwas davon zu erzählen. Die Lehrerin und die zwölf Kinder schließen sich ihnen nicht an. Die gesamte Gruppe verabschiedet sich von dem Anwalt und verlässt das Dorf.

WORDS TO REMEMBER

1. **Ich bin** - I am
2. **Du bist** - You are
3. **Sie ist** - She is
4. **Wir sind** - We are

5. **Sie sind** - They are
6. **Er ist** - He is
7. **Ich habe** - I have
8. **Er hat** - Ha has
9. **Sie hat** - She has
10. **Wir haben** - We have
11. **Sie haben** - You have
12. **Zu** - To
13. **Um ..... herum** – Around something
14. **In** - Within
15. **Auf ..... zu** - Towards
16. **Bevor** - Before
17. **In** - In
18. **Bei** - At
19. **Aus** - From
20. **Mit** - With
21. **Auf** - On
22. **Über** - Above
23. **Von** - Of
24. **Unter** - Under
25. **Unter** - Among
26. **Hinein** - into
27. **Neben** - Beside
28. **Aus** - Out of
29. **Weg** - Away
30. **Vorbei an** - Past
31. **Durch** - Through
32. **Zwischen** - Between
33. **Unter** - Below

QUESTIONS

1. Welches Reisebüro empfiehlt Jack für die Planung der Reise?

- a. Herr Wanderer
- b. Herr Butler
- c. Herr Koch
- d. Herr Google

2. Wer plant die Reise?

- a. Das Reisebüro
- b. Jack
- c. Rose
- d. Der Rechtsanwalt

3. Welche der folgenden Aussagen ist richtig?

- a. Rose hat besondere Gefühle für Jack
- b. Jack liebt Rose
- c. Rose ist Jacks Schwester
- d. Jack und Rose sind Feinde

4. Warum möchte die Lehrerin nicht an der Reise teilnehmen?

- a. Weil sie Rose hasst

- b. Weil sie keine Ferien mag
- c. Weil die Eltern der Kinder wollen, dass sie sofort zurückkommen
- d. Weil die Kinder nicht mitfahren wollen

5. Wie verlassen Jack und Rose das Dorf?

- a. Mit dem Kleinbus
- b. Mit dem Zug
- c. Mit dem Flugzeug
- d. Mit dem Auto

ANSWERS

1. **d.** Herr Google
2. **b.** Jack
3. **a.** Rose hat besondere Gefühle für Jack
4. **c.** Weil die Eltern der Kinder wollen, dass sie sofort zurückkommen
5. **d.** Mit dem Auto

ENGLISH TRANSLATION

Both Jack and Rose look at the map of Italy and the countries around it. There are so many places. They feel confused. They are unable to decide which one, among the various places, is right for them.

"I think using this map to choose a destination is not a good idea," Rose says.

"I agree. What do we do then?" says Jack.

"I don't think there is any travel agent here who can help us."

"There is one."

"Who is it? Do you know their office address?" Rose asks.

"Yeah! He is Mr. Google. And he lives right here, in my pocket," Jack jokes.

Rose laughs. She is amused. Jack opens his phone and begins browsing.

"So we have two days to spare. Do you want to take a one-day trip or a two-day one?" Jack asks.

"Since we both have to travel to Florence, we can take a trip to a place close to the city. After spending Saturday and half of Sunday at our chosen destination, we can travel straight to Florence from there. What do you think?"

"Great idea!" says Jack.

"I am an adventurous person. I love surprises! So, let's do this. You plan the trip, but don't tell me anything now. It will be great fun!" Rose says.

"Are you sure you want to rely on my choice? We barely know each other."

"I'm completely sure. We don't know each other well, but we are not strangers either."

"All right, then! I will do it."

"But please don't include train or plane journeys. We don't want any more delays and layovers. My boss will surely fire me if I don't get to work on Monday morning," Rose says.

"Done! Get ready for the adventure!" Jack says with a wink.

Rose is eager to know where Jack will take her.

"Before I start booking, I think we should ask the teacher and the children if they would like to join us on this trip."

"Uhm... I think so, yes. But I think they will not want to come along with us. The teacher has a schedule that she must follow," says Rose. She doesn't want them on this trip.

"Let me just ask the teacher once," Jack says and begins walking towards the garage. Rose sits down on a rock under a tree and waits for him to return. She has feelings for Jack now. She watches him as he walks beside the row of strawberry bushes and into the garage. She dreams about the trip as she gazes at the beautiful branches above her dancing in the wind.

"He is so charming!" she thinks to herself.

After about 10 minutes, Jack walks out of the garage with the teacher. All the twelve children are behind them and they have their bags in their hands. She looks at the teacher and smiles, but within her heart, she is not happy because she knows the teacher and the children are coming along with them.

"Pack your bags, Miss Rose! We will leave in 30 minutes. We have to reach our destination before nightfall," Jack tells her.

"Oh yes! I am so excited! I will be ready."

Off she goes past the group and into the lawyer's house to fetch her bags. She quickly pulls out her bag from below the table and puts in her belongings. She then runs a comb through her glossy black hair and steps out of the house with her bags. She sees an empty waiting car and a van where the children are seated with their teacher. She looks at the innocent faces of the children and feels sad. She realizes that she was being selfish. She now wants them to come along on the trip. The teacher jumps out of the van and comes running towards Rose.

She places Rose's hand between hers and says, "It was really a pleasure meeting you and spending time with you. I hope to see you again."

"Are you and the children not joining us on our trip?" Rose asks in surprise.

"No, dear. We have to go."

"I have an idea! Why don't you join us for a day and then leave? You have two days before the school week. I think Jack spoke to you about the trip, right? He has planned something really exciting!"

"The school and the parents of these children want us to return immediately. They are worried for the little ones," says the teacher.

Rose hugs the teacher and the children. The lawyer and Jack too, they bid them goodbye. The van carrying the teacher and her students speeds away. Jack and Rose also thank the lawyer for his kindness and hospitality. They load their bags into the waiting car and depart. The lawyer watches as the car travels downhill and disappears into the distance.

CONCLUSION

Congratulations! You have done it!

Reading and understanding a whole story comprising seventeen chapters and several phrases and dialogues in a new language is not easy. Thanks to your efforts, you now know what to say when you meet someone, how to discuss the weather and food, how to ask for directions, how to speak to the salesperson at a shopping mall, how to express your emotions, what to say when you fall in love with someone, and so much more. Through Jack and Rose's story, you have experienced many real-life situations in this new language. You might not have understood each and every word in the book, but what you have accomplished is commendable! You have managed to learn a new language on your own without the help of any teacher and outside of a classroom setting.

Now what?

Now, it's time to practice!

Pick out all those aspects of the book that you didn't understand completely and attempt to master them. Try interacting with a native speaker. Expose yourself to videos, movies, and articles in this new language and try to pick up as much as you can. Every effort you make will take you closer and closer to the ultimate goal of perfection and fluency. No one can learn a language in the space of a few weeks. Even native speakers who are fluent have mastered the language over many years. So, don't feel discouraged. It's normal to find this experience challenging at times, it's normal to forget a few words here and there, and it's normal to make mistakes. Every time you practice, you grow. This gradual growth will eventually take you up there to the pinnacle of success in your language learning journey. Don't give up and don't settle for the ordinary because the best things in life lie on the other side of hard work and patience.

What's next?

There are four books in this series - all packed with short stories and dialogs - that focus on everyday Spanish, ensuring that you learn the basics of the language.

Search for **Language Mastery** to find the rest of the books in the series, as well as dozens of other resources. To continue your language learning journey, simply add the book to your library. We have a book collection, which you can find on your favorite online bookstore or library, that outlines practical steps that you can take to keep learning any language. If you are ever lost or in need of new ideas or direction, we suggest you consult our book collection or just send us an email, we will be there to help you.

Your biggest fan,
Language Mastery!

ALSO BY LANGUAGE MASTERY

SPANISH TITLES

SPANISH 1. **Spanish Short Stories for Beginners:** *Over 100 Conversational Dialogues & Daily Used Phrases to Learn Spanish. Have Fun & Grow Your Vocabulary with Spanish Language Learning Lessons!*

SPANISH 2. **Conversational Spanish Dialogues:** *Over 100 Conversations and Short Stories to Learn the Spanish Language. Grow Your Vocabulary Whilst Having Fun with Daily Used Phrases and Language Learning Lessons!*

SPANISH 3. **Learn Spanish with Short Stories:** *Over 100 Dialogues & Daily Used Phrases to Learn Spanish in no Time. Language Learning Lessons for Beginners to Improve Your Vocabulary & Speak Spanish Like a Native!*

SPANISH BUNDLE. **Learn Spanish for Beginners:** *Over 300 Conversational Dialogues and Daily Used Phrases to Learn Spanish in no Time. Grow Your Vocabulary with Spanish Short Stories & Language Learning Lessons!*

FRENCH TITLES

FRENCH 1. **French Short Stories for Beginners:** *Over 100 Conversational Dialogues & Daily Used Phrases to Learn French. Have Fun & Grow Your Vocabulary with French Language Learning Lessons!*

FRENCH 2. **Conversational French Dialogues:** *Over 100 Conversations and Short Stories to Learn the French Language. Grow Your Vocabulary Whilst Having Fun with Daily Used Phrases and Language Learning Lessons!*

FRENCH 3. **Learn French with Short Stories:** *Over 100 Dialogues & Daily Used Phrases to Learn French in no Time. Language Learning Lessons for Beginners to Improve Your Vocabulary & Speak French Like a Native!*

FRENCH BUNDLE. **Learn French for Beginners:** *Over 300 Conversational Dialogues and Daily Used Phrases to Learn French in no Time. Grow Your Vocabulary with French Short Stories & Language Learning Lessons!*

ITALIAN TITLES

ITALIAN 1. **Italian Short Stories for Beginners:** *Over 100 Conversational Dialogues & Daily Used Phrases to Learn Italian. Have Fun & Grow Your Vocabulary with Italian Language Learning Lessons!*

ITALIAN 2. **Conversational Italian Dialogues:** *Over 100 Conversations and Short Stories to Learn the Italian Language. Grow Your Vocabulary Whilst Having Fun with Daily Used Phrases and Language Learning Lessons!*

ITALIAN 3. **Learn Italian with Short Stories:** *Over 100 Dialogues & Daily Used Phrases to Learn Italian in no Time. Language Learning Lessons for Beginners to Improve Your Vocabulary & Speak Italian Like a Native!*

ITALIAN BUNDLE. **Learn Italian for Beginners:** *Over 300 Conversational Dialogues and Daily Used Phrases to Learn Italian in no Time. Grow Your Vocabulary with Italian Short Stories & Language Learning Lessons!*

GERMAN TITLES

GERMAN 1. **German Short Stories for Beginners:** *Over 100 Conversational Dialogues & Daily Used Phrases to Learn German. Have Fun & Grow Your Vocabulary with German Language Learning Lessons!*

GERMAN 2. **Conversational German Dialogues:** *Over 100 Conversations and Short Stories to Learn the German Language. Grow Your Vocabulary Whilst Having Fun with Daily Used Phrases and Language Learning Lessons!*

GERMAN 3. **Learn German with Short Stories:** *Over 100 Dialogues & Daily Used Phrases to Learn German in no Time. Language Learning Lessons for Beginners to Improve Your Vocabulary & Speak German Like a Native!*

GERMAN BUNDLE. **Learn German for Beginners:** *Over 300 Conversational Dialogues and Daily Used Phrases to Learn German in no Time. Grow Your Vocabulary with German Short Stories & Language Learning Lessons!*

www.ingramcontent.com/pod-product-compliance
Lightning Source LLC
Chambersburg PA
CBHW071911070526
44583CB00016B/1948